10 GOLDEN LAWS TO SUCCESS

Acknowledgement

This study was made possible by the help and co-operation of various people whose effort cannot pass without mention. I therefore want to use this opportunity to register my sincere thanks to them all.

I first and foremost thank the almighty God for his goodness and mercy and for the knowledge and the courage to go through this book peacefully and successfully and also his protection and guidance throughout my research and others.

In appreciation for a life time of fragrance of memories, stimulation of mentality, magnificent in this work, it is upon his shoulders that the successful book was brough into light Mrs. Sarah White; I will always remember every minute you spent with me in the course of guiding this work.

Finally, I express my heartfelt gratitude to my parents and siblings for their financial support, their attention, and understanding.

Thank you all.

Dedication

I dedicate this work to my dear and beloved Guardian, Mrs. Sarah, I say may God bless you for sacrificing for me to this far.

Preface

This book is aimed at helping everyone seek answers to all kinds of question on how to be successful. What are the most fundamental laws to success? What guidelines will help me keep my integrity? How do I do about actually put the laws to together? How can I keep relevant? How do I focus to achieve success? What are the secrets in becoming successful? What are the dynamics of authority? What kind of knowledge should I seek? What kind of people and books I should seek for reference?

People want, even demand, successful knowledge. It is exciting to succeed in life today. I lot of book and bible teachings about success. Pastors always preach about success, and even teachers also teach about success.

Clearly, people in this world are in crisis want to find and live success. People all over the world cry for knowledge about the way to success. A lot of young people are struggle to succeed in live. It is my hope that this book will assist all people; being it old or young in realizing their holistic goal. Accordingly, the book is divided into ten chapters: identifying your natural talent, mastermind, confidence, habit of saving, initiative and leadership, imagination, enthusiasm, self-control, and staying focused. All this law talks about the way of becoming successful. You will become successful if you take these laws seriously and practice them daily.

Martin White

August 24, 2022.

Table of Contents

CHAPTER ONE

IDENTIFY YOUR NATURAL TALENT

Everyone human being is born with natural talent which manifest itself in so many ways some parents are even one aware of their child natural talent. The following are some natural talents everyone has.

- Adaptability
- Perseverance
- Honesty
- Enthusiasm
- Inquisitiveness
- Teamwork
- Entrepreneurship

How to Discover Your Talents

These are some of the ways one can discover their talent.

- **Take a life assessment.**

  No life assessment resembles the other. Every Life Assessment test would be different from the other. If you want to know about your potential in life, take this assessment test.

  Besides being free of cost, it allows you to understand how you perform in different aspects of life. You will be able to identify and pinpoint the facet of life that needs maximum attention.

  Additionally, with the help of such tests, you can realize what makes you tick. The Meyers-Briggs Type Indicator is one of the most promising tools that can help you define your life and personality patterns. It would allow you to check what type of motivations in life are more suited to you.

Once you can judge the category you come into, you can list your strengths and shortcomings more precisely.

You can even use the results of such tests for a walk-in interview, on a date, or any other high-stake situation. Play around with your newly discovered strengths.

- **Find what makes you feel strong.**

Talent identity is all about finding what makes you stronger. When we say stronger, you must be purposeful in life and experience growth and satisfaction. That is what this entire life is all about.

You must have come across situations where everything seems flawless and easy. When you are good at some things, everything appears easier. Our inner sense always draws us to things that make us feel calm and content in life. However, you feel low when you feel out of place or do not really get that satisfaction from your daily life.

These are the times to identify and recall what made you feel good about your life. It might be your talent to deal with kids or play games. Whatever it may be, that would define your strength.

You need to ensure that you pursue such talents, whatever you are good at. If you are good with kids, try babysitting or volunteering your time in any after-school program. That is what would make define your schedule as per your strengths.

- **Find what you spend the most money on.**

One of the best ways to identify talent is by checking where you spend your money the most. If you are not good at maintaining books or records of your finances, try out using free and easy-to-use applications such as Mint. It would allow you to determine where your maximum dollars are spent.

Following your green would lead you to discover your talent. If you check your finances for the past 12 months, you will find a specific spending pattern on certain things. If you spend regular money to keep up with your gym schedule, maybe you are good at it, and that is what your talent is!

Use this discovery of talent to your advantage by going on advanced stages of such activities and enjoying your life to the fullest. This would give you utmost satisfaction.

- **Ask your friends what your best and worst qualities are.**

  Why not retort to talking to the very close people you, such as your family or friends. They are the ones who have been with you for a long time, and these are the people who would undoubtedly know clearly what your passions and interests are. More importantly, they can tell you what you are good at.

  It can be anything from singing to dancing to cracking jokes. Things that come to you effortlessly and entertain others are your talents.

When you ask your friends about your best and worst qualities, ask them to be brutally honest with you. Knowing about your weaknesses or worst qualities helps you isolate such habits or activities from your life. This would only leave you with things that you are good at.

- **Ask your family what you loved as a child.**

  Why not talk to your mother, dad, or siblings and check with them about what you loved when you were a child.

  Maybe you are having difficulty remembering such things, but they would surely remember. These are the people in your life who have known you for the longest.

  There are things and habits that we pick up as kids and try to be good at these. Maybe we were good at it, but we tended to forget such things as we grew.

  Your past behaviors, likes, and dislikes would give you a clear insight into your personality and how you grew up.

  If some of these things still tickle your brain or bring excitement, these were the things that you loved and were good at. That's what your talent is! Try to recreate your childhood and bring back the same level of gusto when you realize your strengths.

- ❖ **Write in a journal.**

  Sometimes nothing works, and we just don't feel like discussing our feelings with anyone. Do you know what is good during such times? Using a pen and paper would be the best companion when you need to be alone and discover your talents.

  Take your journal and let your thoughts go wild. Write something every day in this journal and make it your routine activity. When you allow your thoughts to flow freely, they will direct you to the things you love.

  After about a week or a month, start re-reading your journal. You will realize that numerous things would attract your attention, and you would like to revisit those thoughts.

  Your journal holds the answer to discovering your talents. It would show you what you miss from your life and what you need to do next. It would also allow you to discover what you desire.

  Reading your journal will allow you to list down your strengths and opportunities.

- ❖ **Look for talent in others.**

  Don't force yourself to do so when you cannot dig deep down in your mindset. Take a break and observe others. There are times when the talent of others inspires us. What attracts us could secretly become our talent.

  Sometimes observing others also inspires us to realize that we are good at it. For example, if an article inspires you but you believe you could have contributed to it in a better way, maybe your hidden talent is writing.

  Look out for something that connects to your soul. It should inspire you and make you feel happy and content.

There would be times when the talent of others would make you feel jealous. But worry not, you can use this to your advantage too! You can seek advice from such a person and get help to develop such talent yourself.

- **Take stock of your book/music/movie collections.**

  We live in a modern society full of audio and video content everywhere. If you collect books, music, or movies, this would be a good time to check your inventory.

  Try to mind what type of media you consume. The category of media that you are fond of reflects your clear inclination to enjoy it.

  Sometimes that helps us determine our identity. There are things that light fire in our lives. Our media collection would give us an idea of what we like. If you find a specific pattern towards a particular segment, dig deep into it by finding other related activities.

  Connect with others who follow similar talents. Sometimes even they can guide us through the next steps of discovering the hidden talents.

- **Remember what you have been thanked for.**

  We do numerous deeds in our lifetime. For a few, we are thanked, and for others, we are not. Try to find out the various things you were thanked for in the past. How did it make you feel?

  If you felt good, then try to recollect if doing a similar errand at a later stage also leads to getting "thanks" from someone. When you are thanked for something regularly, you are good at it, which could be your hidden talent.

  You might be a good listener, a good motivator, or a good teacher. These small thank yous' may seem insignificant at times. However, somewhere deep down, these are our talents.

- **Be open to change.**

  Once you have found how to identify talent, be open to change. You might have to make major life-changing decisions after discovering your talent.

It might seem unsettling initially, but that is what would make you happy eventually. You cannot expect to stay stagnant and grow. You need to accept change and do it willingly.

Don't retort to finding reasons to delay or neglect such changes. You need to give yourself a chance to live a life that makes you happy through your talents. You will have to let go of all the preconceived notions and willingly accept the new thoughts and habits. You will find that such changes would make your content and prepare you for more life challenges.

❖ **Select Your Talents**

It might turn out that you are multi-talented. You can be good with more than one thing in life. And this can be a good thing since it proves to be very motivating.

You need to choose from the list of things you are good at during such times. Decide what talent ticks your heart and soul. What makes you happy and content is what you should shortlist and pursue.

Just choose and dig deep into your passions to live a happy and content life.

❖ **Upgrade**

Discovering your talent does not mean that your story of self-discovery has ended. It requires you to constantly learn and upgrade your knowledge and become more proficient to upgrade your skillset.

Take up courses, attend seminars, watch videos, read books, or do anything that will help you with upgrading your talent.

With time almost everything becomes outdated, and therefore you should never be satisfied when it comes to learning and upgrading your knowledge.

❖ **Reach Perfection**

Perfection is constant evolution and up-gradation of knowledge. Flawlessness means to become better compared to the person you were yesterday!

Hustle, question constantly, select your abilities, update and arrive at your compulsiveness. Be the best form of you!

That is how you reach perfection!

Final Thoughts

Life is not always a straight line. It is sometimes zigzag or runs in circles. We need to be aware of our strengths if we need to deal with the ups and downs of our lives. Our strengths give us the courage and vision to fight mental demons and face life's challenges.

Hopefully, you enjoyed reading our rundown of steps that will help you find answers to "how to discover your talent." Let the above pointers guide you to discover your talents.

CHAPTER TWO

SELF CONFIDENCE

Do you want to grow in confidence and maximise your professional impact? Is a lack of confidence holding you back from reaching your goals and fulfilling your potential? Do you sometimes struggle to make yourself heard in meetings or at networking events? Do you find it difficult to build rapport with other people in your personal and professional life? Do you want to take control of your first impression and make a positive impact on everyone you meet?

In business, as in life, you only get one chance to make a first impression, so it is vital to make yours memorable for all the right reasons. If you want to elevate your professional presence and learn how to communicate more effectively, The Polished Professional is the course for you.

Confidence can be a tough thing to build up. We've put together some handy tips to help you out. If you're still having a hard time even after trying these self-help ideas, don't worry! We've also listed the ways you can find extra support and work on boosting your confidence with the help of others.

What is a confident person?

Not everyone is born with an inbuilt sense of self-confidence. Sometimes it can be hard to develop confidence, either because personal experiences have caused you to lose confidence or because you suffer from low self-esteem.

Things confidence person do;

A confident person:

- does what they believe is right, even if it's unpopular
- is willing to take risks
- admits their mistakes and learns from them
- is able to accept a compliment
- is optimistic

How to building self-confidence

There are a number of things you can do to build your confidence. Some of them are just small changes to your frame of mind; others you'll have to work on for a bit longer to make them familiar habits.

1. **Look at what you've already achieved**
   It's easy to lose confidence if you believe you haven't achieved anything. Make a list of all the things you're proud of in your life, whether it's getting a good mark on an exam or learning to surf. Keep the list close by and add to it whenever you do something you're proud of. When you're low in confidence, pull out the list and use it to remind yourself of all the awesome stuff you've done.

2. **Think of things you're good at**
   Everyone has strengths and talents. What are yours? Recognising what you're good at, and trying to build on those things, will help you to build confidence in your own abilities.

3. **Set some goals**

   Set some goals and set out the steps you need to take to achieve them. They don't have to be big goals; they can even be things like baking a cake or planning a night out with friends. Just aim for some small achievements that you can tick off a list to help you gain confidence in your ability to get stuff done.

4. **Talk yourself up**

   You're never going to feel confident if you have negative commentary running through your mind telling you that you're no good. Think about your self-talk and how that might be affecting your self-confidence. Treat yourself like you would your best friend and cheer yourself on.

5. **Get a hobby**

   Try to find something that you're really passionate about. It could be photography, sport, knitting or anything else! When you've worked out your passion, commit yourself to giving it a go. Chances are, if you're interested or passionate about a certain activity, you're more likely to be motivated and you'll build skills more quickly.

Ways To Nourish Your Self-Esteem When It Is Low:

That said, it is certainly possible to improve our self-esteem if we go about, it the right way. Here are some ways to nourish your self-esteem when it is low:

1. **Use positive affirmations correctly**

   Positive affirmations such as "I am going to be a great success!" are extremely popular, but they have one critical problem — they tend to make people with low self-worth feel worse about themselves. Why? Because when our self-esteem is low, such declarations are simply too contrary to our existing beliefs. Ironically, positive affirmations do work for one subset of people — those whose self-esteem is already high. For affirmations to work when your self-esteem is lagging, tweak them to make them more believable. For example, change "I'm going to be a great success!" to "I'm going to persevere until I succeed!"

2. **Identify your competencies and develop them**
   Self-esteem is built by demonstrating real ability and achievement in areas of our lives that matter to us. If you pride yourself on being a good cook, throw more dinner parties. If you're a good runner, sign up for races and train for them. In short, figure out your core competencies and find opportunities and careers that accentuate them.

3. **Learn to accept compliments**
   One of the trickiest aspects of improving self-esteem is that when we feel bad about ourselves we tend to be more resistant to compliments — even though that is when we most need them. So, set yourself the goal to tolerate compliments when you receive them, even if they make you uncomfortable (and they will). The best way to avoid the reflexive reactions of batting away compliments is to prepare simple set responses and train yourself to use them automatically whenever you get good feedback (e.g., "Thank you" or "How kind of you to say"). In time, the impulse to deny or rebuff compliments will fade-which will also be a nice indication your self-esteem is getting stronger.

4. **Eliminate self-criticism and introduce self-compassion**
   Unfortunately, when our self-esteem is low, we are likely to damage it even

further by being self-critical. Since our goal is to enhance our self-esteem, we need to substitute self-criticism (which is almost always entirely useless, even if it feels compelling) with self-compassion. Specifically, whenever your self-critical inner monologue kicks in, ask yourself what you would say to a dear friend if they were in your situation (we tend to be much more compassionate to friends than we are to ourselves) and direct those comments to yourself. Doing so will avoid damaging your self-esteem further with critical thoughts, and help build it up instead.

5. **Affirm your real worth**

   The following exercise has been demonstrated to help revive your self-esteem after it sustained a blow: Make a list of qualities you have that are meaningful in the specific context. For example, if you got rejected by your date, list qualities that make you a good relationship prospect (for example, being loyal or emotionally available); if you failed to get a work promotion, list qualities that make you a valuable employee (you have a strong work ethic or are responsible). Then choose one of the items on your list and write a brief essay (one to two paragraphs) about why the quality is valuable and likely to be appreciated by other people in the future. Do the exercise every day for a week or whenever you need a self-esteem boost.

The bottom line is improving self-esteem requires a bit of work, as it involves developing and maintaining healthier emotional habits but doing so, and especially doing so correctly, will provide a great emotional and psychological return on your investment.

Ways to trick yourself into feeling confident, even when you're not

a. **Think about the days you did feel confident**

   Just like we all have moments where we feel down on ourselves, we also all have moments where we look in the mirror and think, "Dang, I look good." On the days you're not feeling super confident, try to remember that one time you did.

Think about how you felt and channel that energy. ***Michelle*** told INSIDER, "Ask yourself one simple question: 'How would I be acting right now if I was feeling great?' What would you be doing, how would you be standing, how would you be breathing?"

Try to get yourself into that mindset again, or at least pretend you're there.

b. Adjust your posture

Amy Cuddy's wildly popular Ted Talk from 2012 explained the way your posture affects how you feel, using "power poses" as a tip to increase self-confidence. Slumping can make you feel more sad, while sitting up straight and holding your head high can make you feel instantly more powerful.

Michelle told INSIDER something similar: "Changing how you are positioning your body tricks your mind into holding the emotion that you would hold in a more upright posture." The next time you're feeling particularly down, try correcting your posture.

c. Repeat a positive affirmation

Keeping a positive affirmation tucked away in your mind is always a good idea — pulling it out when you need it can help you feel good about yourself. Think of something that works for you. You can look for ideas online or just think up something on your own.

The phrase definitely doesn't need to be complicated or long. ***Michelle*** told INSIDER, "When I feel scared, I say, 'You've got this.'"

Simple as that. Repeat it in your head until you actually feel it.

d. Refuse to talk negatively about yourself

The main reason many of us don't feel confident is that we don't really let ourselves. We are, after all, our own worst critics. There are tons of things we say to ourselves that we would never even think of saying to anyone else (except maybe our worst enemies).

When you feel those thoughts coming on, actively push them away. ***Michelle*** told INSIDER, "I don't actually believe in 'faking confidence' in that if you are acting and behaving confident, then you are confident. While me not talking negatively about myself led to this portal of confidence, and I, in a way, 'faked' it, it also wasn't faking it because when you don't vocalize those thoughts, those thoughts actually [decreased], so I actually was more confident."

Every time you think something bad about yourself, immediately think of something good to counteract it.

e. Learn how to accept criticism

Although most confidence issues come from within, sometimes a particularly bad self-esteem day can come from the way others treat you. You can't let them bring you down all the time. In order to get past this, accept that criticism sucks and learn how to move past it.

Michelle told INSIDER, "It's okay to accept that it made you sad, acknowledge the feeling, and let yourself feel it." Pushing away those feelings is only a band-aid on a larger problem.

f. Practice different breathing patterns

Just like adjusting your posture can change your attitude, so can specific breathing techniques. When you're feeling anxious, you're often told to breathe deeply and slowly to calm yourself down. Something similar can make you feel a little bit more confident at times, especially in nerve-wracking moments.

Michelle told INSIDER, "There is no specific breathing technique here. The question to ask yourself is, 'how would I be breathing right now if I was at my most confident?'"

Think about it, then go from there.

g. **Wear something that makes you feel good**

You probably have one thing in mind that you know makes you feel more confident. Maybe it's a dress you think you look great in, or maybe it's a certain lipstick that gives you a power boost.

Michelle told INSIDER, "I warn away from suggesting clothing items or beauty products to improve your body image, but if there is something you can wear that will make you feel more positive, go for it!"

You shouldn't always be dependent on certain items to feel confident, but if they can help get you there in the long run, work it.

h. **Let yourself have bad days sometimes**

Again, it's important to remember that confidence is a lifelong journey. It won't always be easy, even if you work really hard at it - and that's okay.

If you're having a day where you feel terrible, sometimes you just need to let them happen and move on, pretending they didn't mean anything - and eventually, they won't. ***Michelle*** told INSIDER, "Just because I think something doesn't mean I believe it. I have gotten to a point where I don't fight my thoughts and I let them exist. In doing that, they go as quickly as they came."

CHAPTER THREE

MASTER MIND

A mastermind group is a great place to brainstorm ideas, get feedback, set goals and find accountability so you can actually accomplish things instead of just talking about them.

Mastermind training

Mastermind groups offer **a combination of brainstorming, education, peer accountability and support to sharpen your business and personal skills**. A mastermind group helps you and your mastermind group members achieve success. Members challenge each other to set strong goals, and more importantly, to accomplish them.

How to improve mastermind

One cam improves his/her mastermind group that actually gets result and keep ***everyone wanting to come back for more through these rules***

1. Choose Your Members Wisely.

When it comes to mastermind groups, deciding which one to join or who to invite to yours, is going to set the tone for the months and years to come. Beyond simply trusting these people with intimate details about your business, you need to be able to relate to them on a personal and professional level, too.

When evaluating whether or not a particular mastermind group is right for you, take into consideration these characteristics for each member:

- **They must relate to you on a personal level.** Can you see yourself being friends, or at least spending non-work time with the members of this group? The reality is, you're likely going to spend at least a few hours each month either in-person or online with your mastermind members. If you don't have similar interests, passions, hobbies, or experiences, you're not going to click.
- **They must have similar experience.** If your mastermind group has members who are coming right out of college and others with ten years of experience running their own business, it's not going to work. It'll be very challenging to strike a balance of sharing, and the value gained will be overwhelmingly lopsided. The more experienced members will gradually drift away or begin viewing it as simply a mentoring session, rather than a true mastermind group.
- **They can't be your competitors.** It's not possible to give objective feedback, or trust recommendations when it's coming from someone who you're in direct competition with.

2. Set Ground Rules Immediately.

As soon as you begin forming your mastermind group, it's critical to set a foundation of ground rules for the group to follow. At a minimum, put together a brief, open Google Document that defines clear answers to all of the following questions:

- How often will you meet as a group?
- Which day of the week or month? What time?
- How long is each meeting?
- Is there a limit to how many members can join the group?
- When and how are new members added to the group?
- What's the criteria for evaluating new members?

3. Have a Clear Agenda & Structure for Each Meeting.

It's essential to have a meeting structure that benefits the members of the group. There's nothing worse than wandering aimlessly from problem to problem without any clear boundaries around what should be discussed and when. In my mastermind group, having a mutually agreed upon agenda helps us to stay on track.

We always start with a few minutes of informal catching up that we cap to ten minutes maximum, then give five minutes updates on where we're at with our goals from the last session. From there, we take a deep dive into a specific challenge that one member is having and offer up actionable potential solutions for twenty to thirty minutes. Finally, we wrap up with ten minutes of an open forum to address any major outstanding challenges from other members, state our goals for what we want to accomplish for the month, and book the date & time for the next session.

4. Decide Upon a Group Leader.

In my mastermind group, our leader is responsible for keeping sessions on track, scheduling the next meeting before wrapping up the current one, sending around a brief agenda before each session, and recapping notes with everyone's goals afterward. The group leader is usually the person who organizes the mastermind, recruits new members, and manages the logistics of getting everyone together in-person or online.

5. Share Evenly.

Arguably the most important tenant of a mastermind group that keeps members coming back for more, is putting in place a structure that encourages even sharing. While one purpose of joining a mastermind group is, without a doubt, to help overcome challenges in your own business, it's just as much about stepping back and selflessly helping others accomplish their goals.

Regular practice of pitching in to solve problems that are outside of your typical area of expertise will give you new perspectives and ideas to implement within your own business.

Your mastermind group won't immediately be perfect, but starting by implementing these five rules into the management structure of each session will significantly help keep everyone engaged, benefiting, and coming back for more.

These are the characteristics of a mastermind.

Masterminds have an unusually strong will; they are **tenacious, determined, and resolute**. At times, because of their drive, and intensity of focus, they can often become single-minded, and can be hard driving with others.

What to Bring to Your Group

We naturally **gravitate** towards successful people. It's innate to us. We love successful people even the low-grade celebrities we outwardly hate yet still fixate over. What most of them have-whether real or just a public persona-is ENERGY. Whenever you see them, they are ON! And this is the number one skill they use to attract us to their brand. So, when you join a Mastermind, you need to focus on the seven key Mastermind skills to attract the right kind of participants.

People tend to gravitate to the most friendly, happy, outgoing people in the room. For most of us, this does not come naturally, but like any other skill, we can work at it and make some improvements. Bringing these qualities to your group requires more than just one skill, but rather a toolbox full of attributes.

Passion

They want to see you get excited about something. They want to feel the excitement in your voice, the energy with which you talk about your ideas and goals. To see that you love what you do and that you have an appetite for life itself. Your excitement – It's not quite the same as a passion, but they do go hand in hand. Smiling, laughing, enthusiastic. Do I need to go on? Quantum physics states that we are nothing but balls of energy and you are either giving out energy or taking it in. Which one are you?

Frustration (Within moderation)

Sharing your frustrations is okay. It shows that you are emotionally invested in what you do, which gives people an added layer of opt-in for helping you succeed.

Opinions

Your Tribe wants to see that you can voice your opinion and get involved, either on one side or another. A real mastermind group allows people to go deeper with conflicting advice, alternative suggestions and diametrically opposite opinions from those already expressed. However, you do have to be aware that a certain level of trust needs to be established **before** this can happen.

Expertise

Show people what you are good at within your field or niche. Don't worry if you don't classify yourself as an an expert. It's not always a good thing.

Commitment

Regular commitment is the key to any Mastermind group. Your Tribe wants to know that you will be there for them and follow through with your promises (Commitment). Without regular participation, you won't receive the maximum benefit from the sessions. It's one of the critical skills you need to possess, and it's a habit worth cultivating.

Helping Others

Business is all about helping solve someone else's problem at a price they are willing to pay this is what most of us are doing all day. However, in a mastermind group, you won't be charging for your ideas or problem-solving skills, but instead, provide them for free. Why? Because you're creating a bond and a community that is worth more than just trading your time for money.

Energy

Make a conscious effort to raise your energy level to match the group. On the flip side, if you are naturally outgoing and bubbly, the group should begin to rise to your level. People enjoy watching others smiling, laughing or sharing their information in an upbeat and energetic way. If you feel there is a lack of energy in your group, try and think of something that will improve it.

When I was backpacking around the world, I was on a bus tour of the South Island in New Zealand. As a consequence for anyone delaying the bus, the bus tour had a rule that the last person on the bus had to tell a joke or sing a song. Everyone got on board with the concept (and the bus), and it quickly created a bond and broke down barriers.

If you are already in a Mastermind group, consider trying out a rule like this for your next session.

CHAPTER FOUR

HABIT OF SAVING

Habit is something you do on a regular basis. So, if you want to boost your financial future, it could pay off to put money aside every day, every week, or every month –it's all up to you.

How to cultivate the habit of saving money

Find out what you could do to become better at saving money.

- **Set SMART goals**

Before you do anything, it might be helpful to take some time to think about what you want to achieve. Or, in other words, what are your financial goals? By answering this question, you'll get a bit more direction and planning should be slightly easier. But one thing to note is that not all goals are good goals – some are too vague, and others are way too unrealistic. If you want to succeed in your mission, you may want to set SMART goals.

What are these, you ask? Well, they're goals which are specific, measurable, attainable, relevant, and time-based, and they should help you define the steps you'll need to take in order to get there. So instead of saying 'I need to save to pay for my wedding', try something like 'I need to save $5,000 for my wedding venue, so I'll put $450 in my Cash ISA at the start of every month for a year.' Not only have you got a goal here, you've also got a plan, a time frame, and the possibility to track your progress. However, please note that the figures used above are only examples.

❖ Spend less than you earn

Many people can struggle to limit their spending and could end up spending more than they earn which could make saving impossible. We live in a society where we're encouraged to consume and show off our latest purchases on Instagram – which, of course, it's not necessarily a bad thing if you manage to live within your means, but it can become an issue when you start overdoing it. The danger of overconsumption and instant gratification is that you could lose control and find yourself in debt. So, if you want to limit your spending and claim back power over your finances, setting yourself a budget to stick to could help.

Budgeting may sound like a daunting task, but it doesn't have to be – everybody can do it! A good way to start could be to list all your expenses and deduct them from your total income. The sum you get after this is your disposable income and you can choose what to do with it.

You could, for example, decide to save a bit and use the rest for leisure – it's completely up to you. But the advantage of having a budget is that you get to plan beforehand. Budgeting could encourage you to bring some logic and thought into every purchasing decision you make, and it could help you spot any areas where you might want to cut back your spending. And if you can't be bothered to do it on your own using an Excel spreadsheet, it could be worth looking into money management apps.

❖ Pay yourself first

Many people will save after spending, and whilst it can work for some, this approach may not work for everyone. Say you spend more than usual one month, then you may not be able to put anything aside, and you could be missing out on a month's worth of saving. If you want to avoid this scenario, it could be a good idea to treat your savings like any other expenses and pay yourself soon after your salary goes in, that way you'll be more likely to make a habit out of it – sometimes all it takes is a change of perspective.

- **Consider saving regularly**

If you want to get serious about reaching savings goals, it could be helpful to make it a habit rather than something you do every once in a while. And by definition, a habit is something you do on a regular basis.

So, if you want to boost your financial future, it could pay off to put money aside every day, every week, or every month –it's all up to you. The idea here is to shift your mindset towards forming a saving habit – the more you do it, the more likely it will stay with you.

You don't even need to make huge contributions; in fact, you might want to consider saving little and often to see what impact this might have on your finances. For example, if you save $70 a month in a traditional savings account, after 12 months, you'll have at least $840 in your account. And if you keep saving at the same pace for another 12 months, your pot will be worth $1,680 (minus interest).

Automate your savings

Saving regularly is a great thing to do, but it's also easy to forget. Unless you're extremely good at remembering things, it could be worth automating your savings. By this we mean setting up a Direct Debit transfer going from your current account to your savings account, that way you don't need to think about it. The money goes in automatically, so you can relax and focus on other things whilst your savings account gets fed – what's not to love?

Think about saving the excess

Getting a pay rise or a bonus is always good news, and whilst it's tempting to splash the cash, it could be wiser to try and save the excess. Of course, there's no harm in enjoying the fruit of your hard labour but having more money in the bank account means you could boost your savings if you wanted to.

You don't even need to add loads to see a difference. In fact, even an extra $10per month could do wonders to your savings pot. Let's take our example from above, by putting $70 a month, you would have at least $1,680 after two years. But now say you get a promotion and your salary increases, and you decide to increase your monthly contributions to $80 a month. After 24 months, you would have $1,920 in your pot – that's an extra $240 at the end, without taking into account any interest that you're paid.

Track your finances

Putting money aside and making budgeting a habit can be a great start if you're hoping to save money, but tracking your progress could help make all the difference when it comes to growing your savings even further.

Chances are that you won't get everything 'right' when you first start changing the way you spend, and that's okay. However, by keeping an eye on your finances, you're more likely to spot what might be holding you back from reaching your savings goals. Then, once you know where improvements might be needed, you can adjust your strategy and find better ways to improve your financial health.

The truth is that there isn't only one way to go about saving money and what works for others may not necessarily work for you. Tracking your finances could help you to stay in control of your spending and devise a realistic strategy for you that is based on your personal circumstances and goals.

❖ **Consider the long-term**

When you get to a place where your finances are in shape and you have enough saved, you may want to start thinking about the long-term.

What happens is that things get expensive over time – put very simply, this is what we call 'inflation'. This isn't just something that reduces your purchasing power by causing prices to rise - it could also eat away at the savings in your bank account. This is due to the fact that if the rate of inflation is higher than the interest rate you're getting from your bank, then your savings will lose value over time.

The thing is that interest rates have been low for years now, which can limit the growth of your money over the long-term. If you were to take your savings out in 10, 20, or 30 years, you may realise that you can't afford as much as you could before with the same amount. So, what do you do? Well, you could look for a competitive savings account with higher rates, or you could consider investing your money.

Putting your money in the stock market can be risky, there's no denying it. Since there's no fixed interest rates, you could end up losing money, however, this also means that there's an opportunity for higher returns. In fact, over the long-term, investing could pay off. According to many studies, the longer you remain invested, the more likely you are to make a gain. For *instance,* people who invested in the FTSE 100 for any 10-year period since 1984 have had an 89% chance of making a profit[2].

Joining the investment world isn't a small decision, and it's important to consider your personal circumstances, financial goals, and risk appetite as these will have an impact on how you approach investing.

When you invest with us, you can choose how much you want to invest, and how often, and tell us how you feel about risk so we can find the investing style that suits you. Then our team of experts will do the hard work for you, from picking the right mix of investments to managing your Plan on an ongoing basis. It really is as simple as that.

CHAPTER FIVE

IMAGINATION

Imagination is the faculty or action of forming new ideas, or images or concepts of external objects not present to the senses. The ability of the mind to be creative or resourceful.

Imagination is the production or simulation of novel objects, sensations, and ideas in the mind without any immediate input of the senses. It is an essential ingredient for success, especially for entrepreneurs.

A lot of people try to make imagination complex, but the easiest way to sum it up is as follows:

Imagination = Creating new solutions to problems

Those who use their imagination to succeed are likely to progress rapidly in their business or chosen career. As most people fail to use their imagination for constructive purposes in their business or employment, it is easy to begin to develop your reputation for accomplishing results by using your imagination.

It's about thinking!

How can you develop your imagination? Napoleon Hill goes into great detail in his book about the importance of having imagination and uses a variety of case studies where people have used their imagination. Hill does not spend a huge amount of time outlining how to develop one's imagination, though. So how *can* we develop our imagination?

The reality is that everyone who emerges from childhood has developed an imagination, but we often fail to use it. When we were little we used our imagination to create fun games and ways of doing things.

In 'The Adventures of Tom Sawyer' by Mark Twain, Tom Sawyer uses his imagination. He convinces his friends to paint a fence he's asked to paint by giving them the impression that it was a 'responsibility and a privilege' that could only be entrusted to a select few. These friends wanted to be seen as reliable and able to do it and Tom ended up charging many of them to do so. Later, he sold them back their toys and other items in order to collect ticket stubs from Bible memory verses in order to get himself a Bible at the Church! This was only available to select children who had memorised several Bible verses and had received ticket stubs to prove so.

Imagination comes when we look at problems and turn those problems into solutions with benefits.

Don't be afraid to imagine and try new things. You never know the rewards you may find from tapping your imagination.

Actions:

- Think of a problem you are facing at the moment in your life.
- Try to come up with at least five ways to solve that problem other than the obvious.
- Try one of them and see what happens.
- Always look for possibilities and solutions, even when they seem impossible. Never close your mind once a solution has been found.

Imagination isn't just for kids.

Every business has a goal. In order to achieve your goal, you are constantly analyzing your results, reworking concepts and aiming to achieve a way to hit your goal and new levels of success for your organization. Being in tune with your imagination will thrust your business forward.

To think outside of the box, take constructive criticism, create new ideas and re-use old ideas in new ways is a success trait that will thrust your business forward. To make your imagination productive, You must organize your ideas ensuring that each idea is productive towards your organizations' goal.

It is time to re-embrace your imagination and put it to work for the success of your business!

CHAPTER SIX

INTIATIVE AND LEADERSHIP

Initiative skills refer to your ability to assess a situation and take action without direction from someone else. Initiative is a self-management skill, and purposeful self-management can help you set goals independently and direct the trajectory of your career.

Examples of initiative skills

- Confidence
- Self-management
- Decisiveness
- Problem-solving
- Professionalism
- Conflict resolution
- Adaptability

How to Improve Initiative Skills

The points explain the ways one can improve his/her initiative skills.

1. **Develop goals**

   Developing goals allows you to set your own pace and understand what you want from your career. This helps you take initiative as soon as your employer presents an opportunity without having to think about it for too long.

   this also help you save time by applying for jobs that fit your plan and gives you more time to initiate contact with specific companies or recruiters. You can create a list or timeline of goal you want to achieve and reviewing it every few weeks.

2. **Practice self-confidence**

   Taking initiative means putting yourself in front of others and making a decision, so it's important to have confidence in yourself to make the best decisions for your workplace. You can practice your self-confidence by making smaller decisions with expected outcomes and slowly making bigger decisions with less predictable outcomes. This helps you feel secure in your choices and teaches you how to fix mistakes quickly. In addition, you can do research about topics that may come up at work so you can prepare an answer or solution in which you're confident

3. **Identify opportunity**

   Learn to notice when opportunities to take initiative arise so you can be the first to move and benefit from the opportunity. In the workplace, its important to observe details to notice if there are things you can improve or new projects you can complete. identifying opportunity allows you to take initiative when you notice these things, which improves your performance and reputation with your colleagues. Try to notice changes in behaviour and take notes during meetings to learn the sign of opportunities to take initiative.

4. **Learn from others**

   Your colleagues can teach you a lot about taking initiative. Watch how high-level employees take action and make decisions in your workplace to learn their methods and techniques for taking initiative. To learn more deeply, ask for advice or tips, and consider finding someone to be your mentor. First-hand experience is a great way to learn and practice taking initiative so you can benefit from your skills in your job.

5. **Practice at home**

   Sometimes, improving your initiative skills requires practice, and practicing at home is a risk-free way to build your confidence and understand your response to sudden challenges or opportunities. You may find it useful to practice taking initiative in the comfort of your home or with family and friends.

   Consider creating a list of opportunities and practicing your response to them in the mirror until you feel comfortable declaring your solution or decision. You may also ask family and friends to roleplay work scenarios with you so you can practice responses to unexpected requests.

How to Use Initiative Skills in the workplace

Initiative skills can help you in all aspects of life, but here are some ways you may take initiative in the workplace:

- **Listen to your colleagues**

  Listening to and interacting with your colleagues can help you learn their concerns and identify potential opportunities, like promotions or projects. Observing your work environment allows you to take initiative and address those concerns or pursue those opportunities before others.

- **Do your research**

  Doing research provides you with the knowledge necessary to take initiative confidently and create successful solutions to challenges in your workplace. Researching current projects, changes in your industry and other relevant information prepares you to make decisions and impress your employers.

- **Innovate**

  Innovation is a great way to take initiative and improve your workplace by thinking of new ways to perform your duties. Using creativity and originality, you can create unique ideas before others and implement changes that benefit you, your colleagues and your company.

- **Offer to help others**

  Helping your colleagues and customers is a way to take initiative that benefits everyone and shows your dedication to kindness and positive production outcomes. Try to help others without management asking you to and offer advice, tips and guidance to help them complete their work.

- **Anticipate challenges**

  Anticipating challenges allows you to take action before anybody else and prevent challenges from disrupting your work environment. Consider what challenges may occur for a project or because of an industry change and address potential solutions in team meetings.

How is initiative related to leadership?

Initiative distinguishes a leader because it's not just about doing what is told, but rather finding new ways to do more. If a leader's job is to build progress, then initiative is how that progress can be built. Leaders understand that you have to find new paths and creative modes in order to accomplish something.

CHAPTER SEVEN

ENTHUSIASM

Enthusiasm is a state of mind that inspires and arouses one to put action into the task at hand. Enthusiasm bears the same relationship to a human being that steam does to the locomotive – it is the vital moving force that impels action.

Enthusiasm is one of your greatest assets. It is better than money, power or influence–with enthusiasm you become the master of these. Combine enthusiasm with faith and initiative, and you can move mountains and achieve results unheard of.

Ways to harness the power of enthusiasm

Apply these strategies and you'll have so much energy, you'll be unstoppable.

1. **Follow your bliss.** There is no better way to generate enthusiasm than to be engaged in an activity that you enjoy and to do work that you're passionate about.
   If your current situation is such that you cannot be engaged in the work which you like best, decide what it is that you want to be doing and focus on the fact that you'll be engaged in that particular work at some point in the future. Even if you're not currently standing where you would like to be, you can generate enthusiasm by facing the direction in which you want to go.

2. **Think of the things that you want to attain**. Here's a quote from Hill's "The Law of Success":
   "The home you intend to own, the money you intend to earn and place in the

bank, the trip you intend to take when you can afford it, the position in life you intend to fill when you have prepared yourself, and the preparation itself—these are the things that produce happiness."

Become enthusiastic about these things, regardless of your current station in life. Keep thinking of the time when you'll be ready to turn these things into reality.

3. **Have a plan.** Creating a plan will fill you with enthusiasm to get up each day and follow through on your plan. Driving around without a map–that is, trying to achieve a goal without having a plan–can soon use up all of your motivation. However, when you know where you want to go–see point "1" above–and you have a map that shows you how to get there–you'll be pressing down on the gas pedal and moving ahead at full speed.
4. **Get out of victim-mode**. Nothing zaps enthusiasm faster than seeing yourself as a victim. Look at the following two scenarios:
   - You're constantly thinking: "There's nothing I can do to get the promotion that I want because my boss hates me."
   - You're saying the following to yourself: "I'll never be able to raise the capital that I need for my start-up because banks just won't lend money to people like me."

   If your thinking is in line with the two scenarios above–that is, if you're thinking like a victim–, how can you possibly generate enthusiasm?

   In order to generate enthusiasm, you need to see yourself as a creator. That is, recognize that you can continually take the steps that you need to take in order to get what you want, regardless of what other people, or even life itself, throw at you.

5. **Surround yourself with people who are enthusiastic and optimistic**. Befriend people who will encourage you and challenge you to achieve your goals. Enthusiasm is contagious; when you're around people who are enthusiastic about their lives and about their work, their enthusiasm will rub off on you.

If you can't find people who are enthusiastic, surround yourself with videos and audio programs of people who are enthusiastic.

6. **Stimulate yourself into a state of high enthusiasm**. Hill explains that everyone has something that arouses their enthusiasm-it could be something like the following:
   - Going to museums to admire fine paintings;
   - Listening to music;
   - Spending time in nature;
   - Wearing clothes that make you "look the part";
   - Reading books by authors that you admire; and so on.

   He adds that all people of outstanding achievement have discovered ways and means of stimulating themselves into a state of high enthusiasm. Identify activities or situations that energize you, and engage in them as often as you can.
7. **Ask questions**. the best ways to generate enthusiasm in yourself is by asking yourself questions about your abilities, your ideas, and your progress. Questions stir up ideas, arouse response, stimulate interest, and create desire. That is, they generate enthusiasm. Here are some questions you can use in order to begin generating enthusiasm

8. **Develop the right attitude.** Another method which one can use to order to generate enthusiasm is to have the right attitude. Attitude is getting the right slant on the thing you are doing.

   Prevette explains that when he became a salesman he adopted the attitude that he was creating and developing ideas to help others. This perspective gave him the spirit to sell; he was eager to find ways to fill the needs of others, and to fill those needs well. Here's a quote from Prevette:

   "The right attitude toward your job taps a hidden reservoir of knowledge and experience, and puts to work every available force to aid you in the accomplishment of your goal."

9. **Give all of your attention to what you're doing**. Still another way to generate enthusiasm is by giving your full attention to what you're doing. Prevette explains that doing any job well requires concentration of thought. Integrate your mental attributes completely, pull together, and pay strict attention to what you're doing. Here's what Prevette says:
   "It is not putting in hours, but putting yourself into the hours that wins promotion, earns more money, precipitates an increase in salary and gets you ahead."
   Whatever it is that you're doing, look for ways to pull your attention together and place it fully on the activity that you're carrying out. It's very difficult to generate enthusiasm when half of your mind is on one thing, and the other half is thinking of something else.

10. **Get your energy level up**. It's hard to generate enthusiasm when you feel tired. Make sure that you have the physical energy to be able to generate lots of enthusiasm by getting enough sleep, eating healthy food, and getting regular exercise.

11. **Lower your levels of "bad" stress**. Stress isn't always a bad thing. In fact, if you want to achieve anything noteworthy in life, some tension is necessary. Look at the following:
    - To achieve great things you need to learn and grow; that is, you need to step outside of your comfort zone on a regular basis.
    - To get things done, you need to set deadlines.
      Challenging yourself to try new things and striving to meet deadlines is stressful. However, setting deadlines that you can keep and striving to meet challenges that you can achieve by making some effort, creates good stress. Bad stress is when you're pushing yourself too hard, and you begin to feel overwhelmed and that you're losing control. Bad stress will zap away at your energy and make your enthusiasm plummet. There are many things

you can do to lower your stress levels, such as taking up yoga or meditation, decluttering your mind and your space, prioritizing, and simplifying.

12. **Use your physiology**. If you're trying to generate enthusiasm, use the body posture and the tone of voice that you use when you're talking about something that fills you with excitement. Move and talk as if you're full of enthusiasm, and your emotions will soon follow suit.

13. **Apply your strengths**. Whatever it is that you're working on, you can become enthusiastic about it by applying your strengths. For example, if you're an artist but you're currently doing office work, look for ways to add visual elements to your work. As a second illustration, I had a friend in law school who loved to sing. He applied this strength to the task of studying for classes by turning the law school lectures into songs.

14. **Begin**. Whatever you want to do, begin it. As Prevette explains, the law of nature is the following: "Do the thing, and you shall have the power." Start learning about the topic at hand; the more you know about something that more likely you are to become enthusiastic about it. In addition, set small goals for yourself and begin to achieve them. These small achievements will help you to generate the enthusiasm that you'll need to keep going.

CHAPTER EIGHT

SELF-CONTROL

What is self-control

Self-control is the ability to control our feelings, emotions, and reactions. Many people struggle with self-control. For example, we need self-control when it comes to staying off social media while at work, sticking to a budget, and regulating our sugar intake.

Scientists continue to study the importance of self-control as a force we can tap into for a more successful, satisfying life. Luckily, there's a lot we can do to enhance these abilities.

The ability to keep disruptive emotions and impulses in check is the mark of a seasoned leader.

Ways to increase self-control

1. Find more motivation.

Motivation is important in honing self-control skills. Figuring out what motivates you the most is key to accomplishing your goals. Otherwise, what is all this work for? When you look at the bigger picture instead of every detail needed to cross the finish line, you'll find yourself more motivated to get things done.

For example, when working on a long-term project, it's easy to get frustrated by the many small steps, meetings, and approvals required to finish it. Instead, periodically reminding yourself and others on the team of the end goal can help promote motivation.

2. Get a good night's sleep.

According to an article by Medical News Today, sleep deprivation impacts our brain function, specifically the prefrontal cortex, which handles reasoning, and the amygdala, which regulates emotions.

Executives and managers should keep this in mind: the more you push employees to work extra hours and answer messages and calls all the time, the more likely employees will be stressed and unhappy. As a result, they may end up cutting corners and engaging in unethical behavior.

Do you encourage your team to prioritize sleep? Do you set a good example? Tired workers are not good for business. Take note of when employees are overworked, and encourage them to openly communicate about it so you can support them accordingly.

3. Self-regulate to improve self-control.

Popular views of self-control are that we should try to control impulses, fight temptations, and actively exercise willpower. But how do you do it?

Self-regulation is a great way to increase self-control because it helps you take control of your feelings and actions. Someone who lacks self-regulation can have difficulty dealing with stress, anger, or anxiety.

According to a Very well Mind article, self-regulation helps you better connect to your values and communicate what you need. This can help you feel more at ease.

4. Exercise to increase self-control.

Do you find yourself with no time to exercise? There's good news for you.

Short bouts of moderately intense exercise can help boost your self-control. No matter how busy you are, plan to include a short burst of exercise in your daily routine. Take note of how you feel after exercise, and you may find you have more energy throughout the day.

5. Get digital self-control support.

Accountability is key. There are many ways to outsource self-control support, including apps that you can download to your phone. They can be helpful when meeting a work deadline, ensuring that you never miss a workout, and keeping track of your meals and spending.

6. Understand your emotional intelligence.

Emotional self-control, or impulse control, starts with understanding emotional intelligence. Knowing yourself can help you manage your emotions and impulses.

For example, do you react impulsively to issues? Do you pause to listen to others' feedback? Are you able to stay composed and positive in stressful circumstances? Can you exercise patience in annoying situations? The ability to keep disruptive emotions and impulses in check is the mark of a seasoned leader.

Here are two emotional intelligence assessments to help you increase your awareness: the Emotional Quotient Inventory and the Emotional Competence Inventory.

7. Avoid decision fatigue.

Self-control has important implications for good decision-making. Decision fatigue harms these abilities.

For example, some people prefer not to make a decision at all, while others may make impulsive or irrational decisions. If possible, avoid making important decisions at the end of the day when your brain is exhausted. "Sleeping on it" can be very helpful.

Additionally, automation is your friend. Put at least some aspects of life on default so you have less decisions to worry about. That can mean using apps or simple decisions you make for yourself in advance. Steve Jobs, for example, always dressed in jeans and black turtlenecks. See how you can simplify decision-making with some simple hacks.

8. Set SMART goals.

You can find yourself losing self-control if the task at hand seems unbearable. Setting actionable SMART goals can help you avoid being overwhelmed. "SMART" goals are Specific, Measurable, Attainable, Realistic, and Time-Bound.

Setting achievable and realistic goals can help you build discipline to complete everyday tasks in both your personal and professional life. Accomplishing your dreams, no matter the size, will result in higher motivation and increased self-control moving forward.

The takeaway: Self-control can be improved. Figure out what motivates you the most, keep an eye on the big picture, and establish SMART goals to reach key milestones. Maintain a healthy lifestyle with good sleep and some exercise. When you learn how to have self-control, you'll find it much easier to go about your day-to-day life both personally and professionally.

So much of success and achieving goals is built on good habits, and good habits are often built on discipline, self-control, and the elimination of bad habits. But improving self-control and building good habits is much easier said than done, and it takes a lot of physical and mental discipline to better yourself.

Improving self-control and build good habits

- **Remove temptation**
  We are not wired to consistently resist temptation, a study found that the way most people resist temptation is to remove the temptation. According to a study by the American Psychological Association, “training self-control through repeated practice does not result in generalized improvements in self-control.” So you can stop beating yourself up for not having much self-control, we're not wired for it. So if people are not wired to have self-control, how do disciplined people exist? They remove temptation, creating effortless self-control. Instead of struggling to resist temptation, remove the temptation. Set yourself up for success by managing yourself and your surroundings by

removing temptations. It helps to make decisions automatic and self-reinforcing, so you can focus on priorities and decisions that matter more.

- **Measure Your Progress**

  What gets measured gets managed. According to Psychology Today, monitoring your progress keeps you focused on your goals. Monitoring helps us become experts on our own behavior, and it makes habits less difficult to govern and change.

- **Learn How To Manage Stress**

  Stopping and taking a few deep breaths helps your heart rate slow down, that helps you relax in the moment. Make sure to exercise regularly, eat well and make sure you're getting enough sleep. It all improves focus, cognitive function and your health. You make poor decisions when your blood sugar is low and you are sleep deprived. Exercise helps you sleep better and helps you have discipline with your diet. Learning how to manage stress in healthy ways ensures you have the energy to keep grinding when work and life can feel overwhelming.

- **Prioritize Things**

  Make a to do list for every day, week and month, so when you're feeling overwhelmed, you know you're making progress and doing the very best you can. It makes you feel more in control, because feeling overwhelmed and like things are out of your control only leads to disorganization, stress and wasted time.

- **Forgive Yourself**

  You are going to fail, failing is a part of life. Forgive yourself and move on. Beating yourself up and worrying achieves nothing, it is wasted energy. Winston Churchill once wrote, "Success consists of going form failure to failure without loss of enthusiasm." Eighty percent of achieving a goal is your attitude, and good attitude is a happy worker, and you're going to need to learn how to happily grind if you want to build self-control and achieve ambitious goals.

CHAPTER NINE

STAYING FOCUS

Benefits of staying focused at work

The most clear-cut benefit to staying focused at work is increased productivity. The more time you can devote to a single task, the more efficiently you'll be able to complete it. This efficiency can lead to better work performance, which can positively impact your career trajectory.

The unsung benefit of learning how to stay focused at work is reduced stress. Focusing on one thing at a time and seeing it through to the end is rewarding. It also closes that task out and gets it off of your plate.

Ways to focus better at work

Here are 13 ways you can improve your focus while working:

These essential laws are what you have to practice to be successful

1. Track your mood

Record triggers that derail you and negatively affect your mood. Note what's happening in your body when you start down a path that doesn't serve you.

- Does your heart race, or is it steady?
- Do you clench your teeth, or is your mouth relaxed?
- Does your body cave in on itself, or are you standing firm?
- Do you feel light or heavy?

Notice what environments make you more stressed. If you're happier and more productive, it means that you are more focused.

Devise some strategies to help you manage your triggers.

Mapping your moods can help you see patterns in your thinking and behavior. Daylio is an app that allows you to track your feelings using visual imagery. The app shows you videos that represent different moods. You can match your mood to the images, and the app records them.

Here's a low-tech way to adjust your emotions. Make playlists of your favorite "feel good" music and play them at intervals during the day, especially when you are in low-energy, low mood mode.

A word of caution: If you find your moods and emotions overwhelming and immobilizing, don't wait to ask for professional help.

2. Assess your mental fitness

Take a week to notice the times of day when you are most productive. Attend to your most important tasks during that time. Notice those low-energy times.

Practice mental fitness daily. The app Lumosity helps you exercise your mind with scientifically validated tasks while making them fun.

You can target the skills that matter most to you by taking a Lumosity lunch break.

3. Eliminate distractions

Take control of your technology. Disable your phone at certain times a day. That means turning off notifications from social media or opting for a complete digital detox.

Freedom is an app designed to block distractions on all your devices. There will be no checking Instagram on your device while you're writing that report because the app won't let you.

Reward yourself with 30 minutes, tops, to indulge in surfing.

4. Give meditation and mindfulness a try

Just a few minutes of sitting in silence, listening to calming music, and connecting to your breath will help you become centered.

You'll return to your work calmer and less reactive to negative emotions, pressures, and demands.

Insight Timer is a helpful tool for guided meditations, courses, meditative music, and yoga practices to support your well-being.

Alternatively, you can set timers that remind you to move and breathe at intervals during the day.

If you crave sound, but music is too much for you, try listening to a pre-recorded mindfulness meditation. It adds background noise that doesn't become a constant distraction.

"When you connect to the silence within you, that is when you can make sense of the disturbance going on around you." —Stephen Richards

5. Notice your sleep patterns

Getting enough sleep is one of the best ways to maintain focus.

Do you maintain a healthy schedule for going to bed and getting up? Are you steering away from foods and drinks that keep you awake? Watching the news can be one of the worst things to do before going to bed. When is it ever good news?

Again, there are many apps to help you track your sleep.

The Sleep Foundation recommends WHOOP, Withings Sleep, and Fitbit Versa.

A few other quick tips for improving your sleep patterns include:

- Reading before bed
- Using a guided meditation app just before you sleep
- Reducing your caffeine intake

6. Get your body moving

Take active breaks. Get up and move. Take a walk. Leave the building.

It's also important to take time to stretch your neck, shoulders, arms, and legs. Set a timer on your phone for five minutes, at least five times per day, to stretch. Get yourself a standing desk or try sitting on an exercise ball while working.

If you feel like some face-time, try scheduling a walk or run with a friend. You don't have to go far, even laps around your block or your house are beneficial. Smartwatches are great ways to record miles, times, and distances. But don't use lack of technology as an excuse!

7. Pay attention to what you put in your mouth

Nutrition plays a massive role in maintaining focus.

While caffeinated drinks can raise your energy level for the short run, you're likely to crash when the high is over. Better to eat snacks with complex carbs and fiber found in fruits, vegetables, whole grains, and nuts for sustained energy and concentration.

Try sticking to just one to two cups of coffee per day. This will keep your energy levels more steady and reduce any cloudy jitters.

"Lack of direction, not lack of time, is the problem. We all have twenty-four-hour days."—Zig Ziglar

8. Find a time management solution that works for you

Managing your time effectively will give you time back to take breaks or shift gears between projects.

One method worth trying is the Pomodoro Technique. It involves working on a task for 25 minutes and then taking a 5-minute break before starting the next 25-minute sprint.

These short rest periods are enough time to give your brain a break and step away from your desk. For example, this could be to stretch, walk outside, or grab a glass of water.

9. Set boundaries around your time

At what time of day do you have the most energy? Set time on your calendar for "white space" during that time.

When you have a large project to do, block off a substantial amount of time that will be distraction-free. This is beneficial even if you can only manage to do it once or twice per week.

Set boundaries and expectations.

Let people know when you are not available and when you will respond to requests. Create blocks of time between meetings to reflect and regroup. Be clear about what's realistic for you to commit to.

Set time aside for a short break in between deep work projects, and you'll find that you'll have better focus when you're working on a single task.

10. Reduce your number of meetings when possible

Consider alternative solutions to meetings.

Ask whether you really need to meet. Is there another way to get information that is not time-intensive but still effective?

Ask for an agenda for meetings. Determine whether your presence is needed if your organization allows for the option. Send agendas before meetings that you're running. Stick to a designated amount of time.

11. Practice active listening

Develop your listening skills by paying active attention to what others say during meetings.

Rather than zone out, ask questions. Engage in the discussion to bring value to the meeting or call.

12. Turn off work at the end of the day

Leave each night with a to-do list, then revisit it in the morning.

Determine your top three priorities. Decide what goes in your "parking lot" of tasks that don't meet the criteria. You can determine when you can do those things, perhaps assigning them to non-peak times during the workday.

13. Make time for your social connections

Don't let social connections take a backseat to work.

Ideally, you'll have downtime to be able to bring your best-focused self to all that you do.

Set up phone calls with friends and coffee chats with co-workers.

Play. Schedule it. Commit to your social well-being and ask others to hold you accountable.

Focus is how someone pays attention or concentrates on a particular person or thing. When someone is focused, their attention is centered on a focal point. In terms of the workplace, an employee is focused when their attention is geared toward completing their main goal or objective.

Ways to improve your focus at work

Here are 10 ways you can help to improve your mental focus and concentration in the workplace:

1. **Eliminate distractions**

   You will be more productive and have a better chance of staying focused when you remove anything in your surroundings that might cause interruptions. If feasible, try keeping your phone in a different room or staying offline to minimize distractions and improve your focus overall. Working alone or in a quiet environment will also make you more focused.

2. **Prioritize your tasks**

   If you have a lengthy number of tasks to complete, it can be beneficial to not only create a to-do list, but to also rank each item by its level of importance. This lets you focus on one task at a time, allowing you to methodically work through your tasks instead of simply being overwhelmed and likely ineffectual.

3. **Train your mind**

   Engaging in various brain training activities is a great way to improve your cognitive abilities and subsequently, your ability to stay focused. When you instruct your brain to become more disciplined, you can become more active in paying attention to the task in front of you.

4. **Work in a quiet space**

   When you're working alone or in a secluded area, you're more apt to get more work done. A quiet environment can help you improve your focus as it ensures you won't be interrupted by colleagues or other noisy distractions from your workplace environment.

5. **Try meditation**

   Taking the time to relax, breathe and meditate can greatly improve your cognitive ability including mental focus and concentration. Try practicing yoga to strengthen your ability to concentrate in the workplace.

6. **Exercise**

   Exercising regularly stimulates your brain and keeps it refreshed. Engaging in physical activity will also improve memory capacity and overall concentration. Not only will it help you stay energized, but it'll also give you the extra boost you need to stay focused and on task at work.

7. **Take breaks**

   Taking time for yourself is a great way to avoid burnout. While steadily completing tasks is important, giving your mind time to recharge and relax can be greatly beneficial for your mental health. If you're stuck on a task, walking away for a short while can provide you with a fresh perspective. Taking a break and allowing your brain time to shut down can also provide you with the momentum you need when you return to work and improve your focus on the task at hand.

8. **Get a good night's sleep**

   Sleeping at least eight hours a night is a great way to make sure you're in your best physical and mental state when you arrive at work. Being sleepy causes you to slow down. Getting a good night's rest, on the other hand, allows you to remain alert and awake-especially during the morning hours.

9. **Focus on one thing at a time**

   When you direct your attention toward one sole task, your risk of distraction minimizes. Rather than multitasking, keep your brain actively engaged on one thing at a time. Improve your quality of work and your attention span by focusing on one task first, then moving onto the next.

10. **Allot time to certain tasks**

When determining what tasks you need to complete, consider the length of time you'll need to complete each. Scheduling out your day and exercising your time management skills will help you complete your work more efficiently and help you stay on top of it all. For example, allot 8-10 a.m. to complete task one, 10-11 a.m. to complete task two and so forth.

Learning how to focus by applying helpful tactics to improve your attention span can help you become a better employee. Though distractions are bound to arise, learning how to deal with them as well as determining what will work well for you, are great starting points to consider.

Benefits of staying focused

Staying committed to a central task can be greatly beneficial in the workplace. No matter the industry you work in, working to improve your focus and increasing your attention span can propel your professional success. Here are four benefits of being focused at work:

- **Builds momentum**

  When you stay focused on one assignment, you're more apt to complete it with greater efficiency. Your ability to finish tasks at a quicker pace can motivate you to move onto the next. Knowing you're capable of getting things done will help you stay positive and motivate you to achieve your next goal.

- **Increases productivity**

  The more you're able to stay on task, the more tasks you'll be able to complete overall. Minimizing distractions is a great way to stay in the zone and allow your brain to process what needs your attention. As a working professional, you're more apt to get more work done when you centralize your attention.

- **Reduces stress**

  By staying on task and increasing your productivity, you'll also be minimizing any tension and pressure that's built up. When you're focused on one sole assignment, you're able to check more items off your to-do list and free up more time in your work schedule. Your ability to direct your energy will guarantee you don't fall behind on work and that you aren't rushing to meet deadlines last minute.

- **Produces better quality of work**

  Your ability to focus is instrumental to your success in the workplace. The more time and concentration you're able to devote to one task, the greater the quality of work you'll produce. Not only will you be completing tasks quicker, but you'll also be ensuring they're free from errors.

CHAPTER 10

TAKING ADVANTAGE OF FAILURE

Failure is the state or condition of not meeting a desirable or intended objective, and may be viewed as the opposite of success. The criteria for failure depends on context, and may be relative to a particular observer or belief system.

Failure can make you stronger

Failure doesn't have to be an **"f"** word. It can be a blessing in disguise when we don't allow fear of failure to hold us back from taking steps toward a better life.

It's understandable to have a negative attitude towards failure. However, it does possess a silver lining. Failing at something forces us to acknowledge where we have room to improve. This can make us stronger and more resilient as we advance one step closer to success.

Failure is a only a pit stop. With perseverance, you will make it across the finish line. *Author Stephen McCranie* said "The master has failed more times than the beginner has even tried." We are hard-wired to learn by trial and error, so failure is like our teacher.

Failing frequently helps us to clarify what we need to do in order to get to where we want to be. By embracing this learning process, we grow more likely to take risks and strive for our goals without worrying about the sting of obstacles. In this way, persistence leads to success and setbacks can be viewed as an opportunity to toughen-up. It's a win-win!

While failure can be a blessing in disguise, the fear of failure can easily overwhelm our desires for a better life. Inaction is commonly symptomatic of fear and can leave you stuck, exactly where you are. Staying within your comfort zone and doing nothing may hurt less than being shot down but, in the long run, it's always better to have tried and failed than to have made no attempt at all.

"The truth is that our finest moments are most likely to occur when we are feeling deeply uncomfortable, unhappy, or unfulfilled. "For it is only in such moments, propelled by our discomfort, that we are likely to step out of our ruts and start searching for different ways or truer answers." according to Psychiatrist and best selling author, M. Scott Peck.

Perfecting a skill through trial and error – whether it's cooking, building something with our hands, turning a car or anything else – is different to falling flat on your face. It took Thomas Edison 3,000 attempts to create what has become the modern light bulb and his legendary grit only made his success more satisfying – and inspirational. Edison approached this project with the mindset that each setback was simply an opportunity to refine his ideas. If his plan had been to complete the project by lunchtime, then he may have given up, like many of his contemporaries.

"Success is 99% failure," says Soichiro Honda, founder of Honda Motor Company.

Take a look at the goals you want to achieve. It might be making more money, getting a license, writing a bestselling novel (ahem), or anything else. Ask yourself, "Why haven't I achieved this yet?" Is fear holding you back? If so, what can you do to manage the negative emotions that come with experiencing a setback? To motivate yourself, can you spell out exactly why you're aiming for this goal?

Keep in mind that all winners fail before succeeding - Michael Jordan was cut from his high school basketball team and Walt Disney was fired from a job because he lacked imagination.

Remember, the more hard-won the prize, the sweeter the victory.

REFERENCE

Bruna Martinuzzi (2022), 8 easy way to increase your self-control

Grant J Everett (2020), failure can make you stronger.

Jessica Booth (2018), 8 ways to trick yourself into feeling confident, even when you're not.

M. Scott Peck, The Road Less Traveled: A New Psychology of Love, Traditional Values and Spiritual Growth

Amy Cuddy's, wildly popular Ted Talk from 2012

https://www.lifehack.org/articles/productivity/10-ways-identify-your-talents-and-utilize-them.html

https://www.forbes.com/sites/francesbridges/2018/06/28/5-ways-to-improve-self-control/

https://www.wealthify.com/blog/how-to-cultivate-the-habit-of-saving-money

https://www.insider.com/how-to-be-more-confident-2018-1#let-yourself-have-bad-days-sometimes-8

https://ideas.ted.com/5-ways-to-build-lasting-self-esteem/

https://au.reachout.com/articles/how-to-build-self-confidence

https://www.thesuccessalliance.com › what-is-a-mastermind

https://eccountability.io/resources/7-key-mastermind-skills/

https://keirsey.com › temperament › rational-mastermind

www.ingramcontent.com/pod-product-compliance
Lightning Source LLC
LaVergne TN
LVHW080817170826
845678LV00011B/2051